APR 1 5

Tell Me Why

WHY?

Penguins Can't Fly

Susan H. Gray

Published in the United States of America by Cherry Lake Publishing
Ann Arbor, Michigan
www.cherrylakepublishing.com

Content Adviser: Dr. Stephen S. Ditchkoff, Professor of Wildlife Ecology,
Auburn University, Auburn, Alabama
Reading Adviser: Marla Conn, ReadAbility, Inc.

Photo Credits: © PathDoc/Shutterstock, cover, 1, 21; © xavier gallego morell/Shutterstock, cover, 1, 15;
© michaeljung/Shutterstock, cover, 1, 5, back cover; © Fredy Thuerig/Shutterstock, cover, 1, 17; © BMJ/
Shutterstock, cover, 1, 7; © TOMO/Shutterstock, cover, 1, 13; © Kevin Lings/Shutterstock Images, 5;
© bikeriderlondon/Shutterstock Images, 9; © Bildagentur Zoonar GmbH/Shutterstock Images, 11;
© Micha Klootwijk/Shutterstock Images, 15; © John Carnemolla/Shutterstock Images, 19; © Anton_
Ivanov/Shutterstock Images, 21

Library of Congress Cataloging-in-Publication Data

Gray, Susan Heinrichs, author.
 Penguins can't fly / by Susan H. Gray.
     pages cm. -- (Tell me why)
 Summary: "Offers answers to their most compelling questions about that
flightless bird. Age-appropriate explanations and appealing photos.
Additional text features help students locate information and learn new
words."-- Provided by publisher.
 Audience: K to grade 3.
 Includes bibliographical references and index.
 ISBN 978-1-63188-010-0 (hardcover) -- ISBN 978-1-63188-053-7 (pbk.) --
ISBN 978-1-63188-096-4 (pdf) -- ISBN 978-1-63188-139-8 (ebook) 1.
Penguins--Juvenile literature. I. Title.

 QL696.S47G73 2015
 598.47--dc23

                                       2014005726

Cherry Lake Publishing would like to acknowledge the work of The Partnership for 21st Century Skills.
Please visit www.21stcenturyskills.org for more information.

Printed in the United States of America
Corporate Graphics Inc.
July 2014

Table of Contents

Walking, Walking

Michael plopped down on the couch and grabbed the remote control. He turned on the TV and clicked from channel to channel. Suddenly he stopped. There was a show about penguins. Michael was hooked. He watched the birds as they swam and caught fish. He loved how they could slide on their bellies. He saw how they walked for miles and miles. "Why do they keep walking?" he wondered aloud. "Why don't they just fly?"

LOOK!

Why would this penguin have trouble getting off the ground?

Penguins are birds, but they don't fly.

Michael was asking some good questions. He knew that penguins were birds. He also knew that birds were supposed to fly. Robins, cardinals, and blue jays were always flying in and out of his backyard. And geese flew in to visit his grandfather's pond. So why couldn't penguins fly like other birds? What was their problem?

Emperor penguins are the largest of all penguins.

No Problem!

Penguins don't mind that they cannot fly. They live on the ground. They don't need to fly. They need their wings for something else.

Many penguins live in icy areas, near very cold seas. It's too cold for most plants to grow. So there are no seeds or berries for penguins to eat. No earthworms live in the ice. So these birds can't eat worms. But out in the sea, food is everywhere. Penguins love to eat fish, **krill**, and squid.

Penguins find their food in the ocean.

Some penguins make their homes in warmer areas. They live on islands or along the seacoast. Either way, they are not far from the ocean. And that means plenty of food. Penguins need their wings to swim after it.

These penguins live in a warm area along the seacoast.

Swimming Champs

In order to catch their food, penguins have to swim. Their bodies are perfect for this. They are smooth and rounded. They are **tapered** at both ends. They easily slide through water.

Penguins have tufts of soft **down**. The down **insulates** the birds. It keeps them warm in cold water. The feathers are packed closely together. They are also a little oily. These feathers keep cold water away from the birds' skin.

Penguins are excellent swimmers.

Before going underwater, penguins quickly breathe in and out. Finally, they take one deep breath and dive down. Most **species** of penguins stay underwater for less than 60 seconds. But some penguins can stay down for several minutes.

Penguins with long, thin bills are experts at capturing fish to eat. Those with shorter bills are great at catching krill. A penguin's tongue has barbs that point backward. These barbs keep slippery **prey** from getting away.

What if a penguin's tongue had no pointy barbs? Do you think they would eat different kinds of food?

A penguin's tongue is helpful when hunting fish.

A penguin's wings are great for swimming. Because they help move the bird through water, they are usually called flippers.

A heavy penguin skeleton pulls the bird down in the water. While other birds are busy flying, penguins are busy swimming. Their food is right there in the ocean.

Other birds have lightweight skeletons. This lets them lift easily into the air. These birds fly from place to place searching for food.

Webbed feet help a penguin swim.

Penguins Are Not Alone

Penguins are not the only birds that cannot fly. Ostriches are also stuck on the ground.

Ostriches travel by running or walking. They have strong legs and big, sturdy feet. They use their wings for balance when running. Ostriches eat plants, bugs, snakes, and lizards. Their food is all on the ground. They don't need to fly.

Like penguins, ostriches don't need to be able to fly.

Other birds, such as kiwis and emus, are also flightless. They have wings but cannot even fly short distances. Still, they manage just fine.

Many zoos have penguins, ostriches, and emus. Some **aquariums** also have penguin exhibits. People can watch them hop about and go swimming. Zoos and aquariums are great places to learn about these birds!

ASK QUESTIONS!

What else would you like to know about birds that don't fly? Ask a teacher or librarian for tips on how to research birds that don't fly.

These macaroni penguins live in an aquarium.

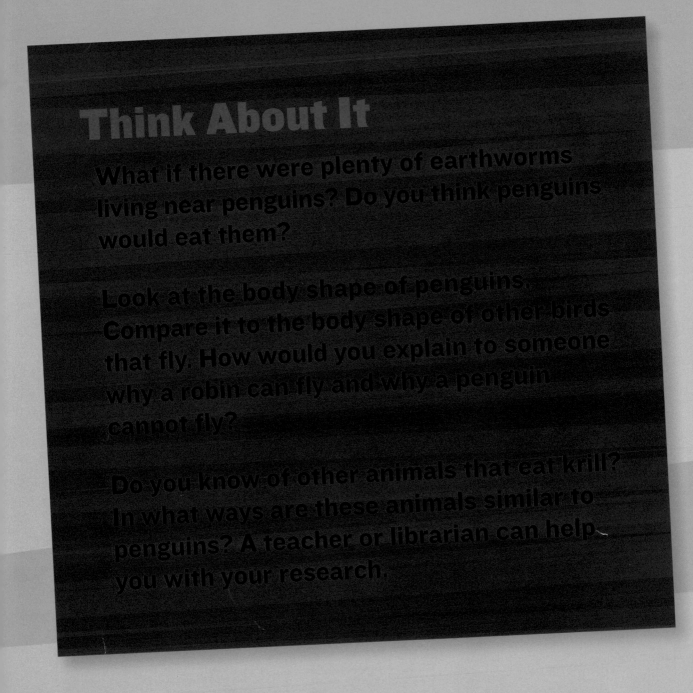

Think About It

What if there were plenty of earthworms living near penguins? Do you think penguins would eat them?

Look at the body shape of penguins. Compare it to the body shape of other birds that fly. How would you explain to someone why a robin can fly and why a penguin cannot fly?

Do you know of other animals that eat krill? In what ways are these animals similar to penguins? A teacher or librarian can help you with your research.

Glossary

aquariums (uh-KWAIR-ee-uhmz) places where underwater plants and animals are on display

down (DOUN) the soft feathers of a bird

insulates (IN-suh-layts) keeps something from losing heat

krill (KRIL) small shrimplike animals that live in the ocean

prey (PRAY) animals that are hunted and eaten by other animals

species (SPEE-seez) a particular type, or kind, of plant or animal

tapered (TEY-perd) narrow or pointed at the end

Find Out More

Books:

Lynch, Wayne. *Penguins!* Buffalo, NY: Firefly Books, 1999.

Schreiber, Anne. *Penguins!* Washington, DC: National Geographic Society, 2009.

Simon, Seymour. *Penguins.* New York: HarperCollins, 2009.

Web Sites:

California Academy of Sciences—Penguins
www.calacademy.org/webcams/penguins
Live penguin cams let viewers watch penguins dive, swim, feed, and hang out.

Kidzone—Penguins
www.kidzone.ws/animals/penguins
A site with facts, worksheets, activities, and do-it-yourself booklets on penguins.

National Geographic Kids—Emperor Penguins
http://kids.nationalgeographic.com/kids/animals/creaturefeature/emperor-penguin
Facts, photos, and a short video about emperor penguins.

SeaWorld, AnimalVision—Penguins
http://seaworldparks.com/en/seaworld-sandiego/AnimalVision/ViewAnimals/Penguins
Another live cam with an excellent view of penguins swimming deep underwater.

Index

About the Author

Susan H. Gray has a master's degree in zoology. She has worked in research and has taught college-level science classes. Susan has also written more than 140 science and reference books, but especially likes to write about animals. She and her husband, Michael, live in Cabot, Arkansas.